THE HAWK TEMPLE AT TIERRA GRANDE

～

Poems by
Ray Gonzalez

～

AMERICAN POETS CONTINUUM SERIES, NO. 72

BOA Editions, Ltd. ～ Rochester, NY ～ 2002

First Edition
02 03 04 05   7 6 5 4 3 2 1

Publications by BOA Editions, Ltd.—
a not-for-profit corporation under section 501 (c) (3)
of the United States Internal Revenue Code—
are made possible with the assistance of grants from
the Literature Program of the New York State Council on the Arts,
the Literature Program of the National Endowment for the Arts,
the Sonia Raiziss Giop Charitable Foundation,
the Halcyon Hill Foundation,
as well as from the Mary S. Mulligan Charitable Trust,
the County of Monroe, NY,
and The CIRE Foundation.

See page 108 for special individual acknowledgments.

Cover Design: Lisa Mauro / Mauro Design
Cover Art: "Luz Misteriosa," by Fernando Mercado
Interior Design and Typesetting: Richard Foerster
Manufacturing: McNaughton & Gunn, Lithographers
BOA Logo: Mirko

LIBRARY OF CONGRESS CATALOGING-IN-PUBLICATION DATA

Gonzalez, Ray.
    The hawk temple at Tierra Grande : poems / by Ray Gonzalez.
        p. cm. -- American poets continuum series ; no. 72)
    ISBN 1-929918-20-8 (paper : alk. paper)
    1. Hispanic Americans--Poetry. 2. Southwestern States--Poetry. I Title. II. American
poets continuum series ; vol. 72.

PS3557.O476 H3 2002
811'.54--dc21

                                                    2001037973

State of the Arts

NYSCA

NATIONAL
ENDOWMENT
FOR THE ARTS

BOA Editions, Ltd.
Steven Huff, Publisher
Richard Garth, Chair
A. Poulin, Jr., President & Founder (1976–1996)
260 East Avenue, Rochester, NY 14604
www.boaeditions.org

To my family in El Paso

Contents

Part Three   ⁓

Part One

Birthday

When Cortés burned Mexico City,
stars glittered black in the sky
before centuries of white light,
four million birds scorched in Aztec aviaries,
conquistadores laughing as their torches
set the moon of feathers aflame, the stench
turning the lake into the next world,
clouds of amber calling to the birds
to come alive centuries later,
rolling across the city as if
water could rise without wings,
without touching everything that flies.

I saw the burning city
several weeks after my birthday,
flew overhead in a plane,
looking down at the streets
I had known long ago.
The burning city ate itself,
miles of smoke and fire cleaning
what had refused to go.

When Cortés burned Mexico City,
brown faces came out of the water,
fled toward the sacrificed heart,
four million birds dropping into
mounds of breathing earth,
taking their time vanishing
from my swollen hands.

When I burned the house of my father,
the color red turned brown,
gave me time to come back.
When I burned the house of my father,
no one was there.

No one knew I was there.
I loved the burning city
several months after my birthday.

Fray Marcos de Niza Erects a Cross at Hawikah (Zuñi Pueblo), 1539

Fray Marcos, your sons are dead,
their faces pointing to the moon.
Your great cross burns the rocks,
takes you to the place God promised
when you were born.
The people watch you dig and
place stones around the heavy timber,
the cross you are glad to leave here.

When they come for you,
you do not resist the arrows in your back;
wait for the cross to light your path.
When they cut your guts out,
you bless them one last time,
watch them climb the cross and wave
your head in the air as you die.

Fray Marcos, you brought God and
the walls of Hawikah burst into flames.
When the people tore the cross to pieces,
splinters lit the ground for nights,
bees of fire driving them away.
Years later, when the others found your remains,
they knew it was you and crossed themselves,
turned around without setting foot
in the abandoned hives of mud.

~

The Scorpions of Coronado

Like red fires conquering the eyes,
the scorpions of Coronado arrive at night,

enter the mind to take a drink,
the bitten body coming to life.

Tails of wind and the one chance.
When something moves,

Coronado marks the trail and comes across,
the scorpions alighting on this side,

aiming their eyes over mountains
where men prosper.

Like breasts moving to please,
the scorpions emerge from

the kiss as the zenith of flowers,
sting the air with the skin of the hour,

press their tails into the sand to see.
Forgotten moment when the foot of prophecy

steps on the wrong path
and the world opens

its rivers of salt, the bitten men
fleeing before the scorpions of Coronado

reappear in the furious night
of swollen stars.

Abo National Monument, New Mexico

a kiva is a Pueblo ceremonial room

Kiva sound.
Juniper smoke ring trashing the sky.

The church at Abo red-rocked to reflect the sun.
Kiva sinking deeper, the wrong habit of soil taking it down.

Ruins for the sake of fighting time,
not letting them go because we need to know

how the low walls transcribed death upon death,
neat rows of corn fighting the morning mist

as if what burned here once would burn again
and the child struck down by the priest went unnamed.

Kiva hole.
Huge cuts for windows where the vision came.

Park fee, museum glass, rattlesnake warning,
tourist camera, the lone trail mistaken for rope

to tie around the waist, descend
to prove the excavated place in the ribs

is the room filled with teeth and worms,
the oven of hunger sizzling with oil

that stayed in the walls until the first scraping,
what was sliced out of the body.

Kiva trash.
Tumbleweed and newspaper holding the bricks.

Manicured walk with printed signs that tell stories,
straining the neck to look up

where the top of the steeple never came down
before the face spotted there vanished in cold rain.

Abo echo.
Abo shoe in the dirt and the pamphlet to explain

why mound after mound surrounding the place
stays untouched, fat treasures covered in grass,

the sudden spot of deer disappearing like
several hundred bodies buried there,

the quick flash of deer turning the sun around,
asking for silence when silence is a stone knife

still embedded in the wall because no hand
can reach up there without bringing the earth down.

~~

The Wide-Open Eyes of the Cathedrals

The wide-open eyes of the cathedrals watch you
enter without falling to your knees,
keep you in shadows until a white beard
grows on your face, your destiny
clear in the unblinking eyes
of what you have prayed for.

The wide-open eyes of the cathedrals draw you
to their light, your wish for blindness
mistaken for holy sight, gift for seeing
what has always been there replaced
by the desire for closed eyes.

The wide-open eyes of the cathedrals let you
come closer so they can cry inside your soul,
but they are stopped by your hypnotic
words of love, the stealth involved
in groping in the dark.

The wide-open eyes of the cathedrals close,
unable to find you as you cross the empty rows,
turn your back on the dying candles,
avoid kneeling before the great forehead that
sweats and sways, wise eyebrows arching
for a silhouette that was never there.

There Will Be Centuries

after Thylias Moss

Pianos will be moved from house to house,
giant machines trembling at the hands of the composers.

Men will climb out of white cars
in parking lots where miracles have happened.

There will be tiny lizards clinging to the chests of boys,
so they aren't captured by cold hands and killed.

Goats will be slaughtered by uncles tired of drinking
and burning their tongues on the naked backs of their mistresses.

Spaceships will hover in the dreams of children taken
by their parents and shown where the light comes from.

Riddles will be shipwrecked
on the pure enamel of a fingernail.

The owl will fly as a prisoner of its own silence,
teach us how the hole in the saguaro where it lives

is the center of a darkness
the approaching century cannot claim.

Mutating computer viruses will become actual beetles,
soft wires turning to green and blue lines populating

the house the lovers abandoned, their transparent wings
buzzing the air of the woman as she flees,

armies of them giving the man time to dress
before they surround him with sound.

The white iguana will be captured
in the millennium photo, where those who love

these things give up wanting to see them,
give in to the inflated chest of the lizard,

its red bubble ballooning to the size of a brain
the refugee claimed when he entered the country.

There will be weeping in silence, what I am saying
mistaken for a postcard left on a table.

Lalo Jimenez will join Juan Sanchez as the first explorers
found alive in the mighty river, their notes mentioning

the two-head salamander without one word
about what was cut out of their hearts,

like the puma that consumed their mothers,
the claws collected years later by their fathers,

their grandmothers, and Cabeza de Baca walking
out of a desert named Chihuahua.

Onmo

The objects that fashion intervention
demand retraction before the feet proceed.
When done, the sobbing takes years to stop.
There is no mention of attempts to hear
the quiet notes rising from the piano.

It is a matter of panicked desire—a puckered
humming from a mound of earth
where the white gowns are prepared
for the lifting of their shapes—
one look at the bodies beneath
and threads of language are formed.

The accordion strikes the bell
and objects are examined by diversion,
the virtues of several witnesses.
Perpetual motions threaten the weather
but the earliest retraction is accepted
by the sound of wounded subjectivity.

There are intimate meditations going on
at the same time this is revealed—
long ago, two objects were given the names
of *sword* and *fish*. No one laughed.
It was easy to have faith in a souvenir
of an awakened man, his messed hair
standing straight to catch radio waves
sent fifty-five years ago when mushroom
clouds settled across the universe.

The objects willing to radiate past
this history demand intervention
when the birdcage is left open
and nothing is the same.
When this is realized, the sobbing

has already become a small cinder
glowing behind a Yaqui mask
mounted in the museum.

Immigration

My loved ones forgotten in the wind with
caricatures of poverty adorning their necks.
They kiss one another, build gallows for themselves,
leave the frame to vanish in the dust.

Collect their amulets and worn sandals outlined
by the English Only crowd mistaking their state
for the land of vision and petrified cars
burning their expensive gasoline.

The wild landscape where my loved ones hide.
It is part of a strong man's hairy chest—
red welts where he gave himself a kiss
when he found a sanctuary for their kind.

Organize the wise believers to follow you
to the edge of the flowers where the bees
tremble and wait to surround the children first,
their hives smashed open by a secret treaty.

Gleaming wishes make it easier to believe
someone will rescue them, take them home,
replace their desires with a yearning for what
never dies, only counts border weapons plants.

You assemble the heart first,
the mind second, their peaceful sleep third.
When you greet my loved ones, nothing
happens without my kindest permission.

This means penance and a way to get there—
Bullfighters on the computer screen flying around
the bull that snorts and screams, its bloody
foam the volcano of my loved ones' dreams.

Mislyxtla Trace

mislyxtla—sweat stains on adobe walls,
their size and the fact they don't disappear
marking the history of a dweller's labor

To those unwanted before they breathe
the looming sound beside thriving engines,
appearance, appetite swallowed by century-ending figures

mistaken for lone rangers applying sin invented by those
getting out with dollar bills, fresh volumes of love
and understanding uncovered beneath torn floors,

anthropological dance broken when Rio Grande floods
caused wisdom to dry into the cottonwoods instead
of mud villages doomed in their distribution,

bright feathers worn without masks,
painted eyes watching you crawl toward the corn,
wiped sweat from traces of sorrowed beliefs—

feet, toes, wombs touching kiss upon cool brown skin
left over from ceremonies for the unwanted before they breathe
the thriving fields green with onions, chilies, lettuce,

roads brown with history snakes, mistaken vultures eating
adobe after running out of dead rabbits hit by startled tractors
demanding the harvest turn into kitchen tables

marked by burned pans, piles of nutrition mistaken for
lifesaving moments, dishes found in the rubble not used,
recipes surviving agricultural landscape, growth labor,

poison air, fresh boxes packed for shipping to those unwanted
before they breathe, belly buttons opening, cutting workers
who fasten themselves to the dust and sing.

Erosion

Inside orange and black rings,
   there is a brown face with closed eyes.
At the edge of a green wall,
   a tiny man with a bald head
lifts his arms and waves.
   Below the red earth of an eroding mountain,
a sister recognizes her brother.
   Among the brown vines of a yellow world,
two women hold each other and cry.

Outside the waves of an ocean,
   a black bull with a white face snorts
before the continent chases him down.
   A man from another country steps into light
and prays he is done,
   says it will rain forever
and believes he has told the truth.

Beyond what I am able to hear,
   small splinters possess my hands,
hold them against the door
   until I believe that man.
Inside orange and black rings,
   there is a brown face with closed eyes.
   Against the brown wall of marble,
the shadow of an angry god
   wakes before the end of the century,
several decades too late to do
   anything about radioactive rosaries,
coal fires outlining the river
   where he destroyed the human race.

Within the circle of tree frogs making
   their way across the border,
there is a spot where nothing moves,

nothing is born, nothing looks
like it came out of a basket of rain—
    spilling water to keep amphibians alive.
Beside the son who lives a crazy life,
    the man he might be stands
against the wind and says something
    to the boy to calm him.

Inside the orange and black rings,
    there is a brown face with closed eyes.
It stares with its vision shut,
    sees everything I have missed.
It will open its eyes when all this stops.
    Someday, when it blinks,
it will be easy to throw seeds
    and pretend they grow,
the orange and black rings of the drum
    the only things to survive the open eyes.

Tiny Clay Doll with No Arms

Given to me by my sister as a gift,
the tiny Indian doll stands with no arms.

Given to me so I can raise my hands
and stop the world from getting closer.

Something has been taken from here—
a day when reaching out was death.

Something lost
with my own hands.

The doll stands three inches tall,
its brown head wrapped in a red scarf.

No arms, as if I could look at a body
and not welcome it back.

As if I knew what happened
to my grip on those things.

The clay doll stands on my bookshelf.
It stares out the window.

It does not have any arms.
I don't know why it was carved that way,

don't know what it means,
why the invisible palms hold everything.

When I touch it with a fingertip,
it leans against a book.

It does not fall.
When I set it back

on its bare feet,
I carefully use both hands.

Time Capsule

It's late. I've come
to love the closing canyons,
placing ground beyond my feet,
burying what became unbraided
in the years of passing this way.
It's late. I've chosen
the back entrance to a wider fear,
the place where I hide things
that must survive—
sequins from the sobbing lanterns,
those basilicas of wax I was given
when hiding the roots of things
was hiding what I feared.

Save the aroma and hide the mestizo,
his arms of corn and cloth of gold.
Hide his bowl of black seeds,
but save his markings.
They belong on the broken church door.
And, the yellow sheets of paper where
I learned to talk to him
by writing what I had to shape,
wavering in the cities like a lover
carrying words on his chest.
Yellow sheets to squeeze into balls
I tossed into a slow barb where
a historical marker in the canyon
will be torn down someday.

Choose the punished mimosa,
tearing branches and leaves, tying them
into a bundle for the other tree—
the only thing to stand beyond
what I am making disappear,
embracing these fists of twigs

to say my nourished kindness
was not said, but spoken to,
those brittle bells of ocotillo
thorns that rang in the wind
of century's end, saving them
to teach me an alphabet,
the sound of bone upon bone
staying in the mind when there was
nothing else to give.
These things I take and hurry away,
not asking for a box or vase, the clay
of yesterday shattering without holding
a generation of anything,
gathering what I need in an armful
of cloth, the shirt from
the mestizo who told me
his galaxy was buried in the ground
long ago, hidden like a bursting hive
of killer bees that never revealed
where they came from, didn't kill
without a chance to know
time from time, canyon from canyon—

the measure of what we hold
as half honey, half bone,
pounds of masa leaves
that will remain after he forgets
where he buried his soul.
These things I evacuate
before my own forgetting.
These things I hide to stay silent,
find the right digging before
I admit I will stay here until
they are dug up and identified.

It Was a Turtle

It was a turtle moving slowly toward the eyes
of an inaudible whisper—what we bring.

It was a turtle moving inside the arms as if skin
were transparent and could answer riddles,

devour secrets like tiny flies evaporating
in its snapping jaws—fumes from flowers,

digging nests for eggs touched
by wormlike fingers,

the husband crawling toward wrinkled layers
of the amphibian who let him out of his skin.

It was a turtle resembling the canoe moving up the arms,
crossing the vein in the elbow to shine on the lake.

How was it mistaken for a knot of thumbs?
Did it hiss when the foot pressed on its shell?

It was a turtle vibrating toward the cove
where claws are cleaned to breathe.

When the firefly streaked into the trees,
it sparked where nothing emerges,

flashed over the head of the turtle that resembles nightmares
where men are frightened into being themselves.

When waste surrounded the abandoned village, these men
found burned turtle shells in cold campfires.

One turtle escaped inside the moss of a horn.
It is the sound of a vowel and a place to see,

the turtle building upon silence that ends here.
When it moves, something floats in the air, then disappears.

Pictures of a turtle returning across the water.
The coin of misunderstanding finding its tracks in the mud.

When the retracted head becomes illusion, it is replaced.
When the shell is preserved, a head emerges with one stone syllable.

Lizard Man

No one knows where the lizard man lies.
He should be the first thing you see when you wake.
In the border town, a hallucination to inspire thought.
The flashy tail was a kite, a lightning bolt hitting
the arroyo to fertilize the witness.
It could be the fever on the cross.
In the *frontera*, we have beliefs
to sweat our bodies dry.

The lizard man loves the owl.
It escapes from his arms, enters
the saguaro and never comes out.
No one knows what the lizard man believes—
the difference between myth and the story
we were told to scare us for life.

The flash of green and the earth unchanged.
The hiss and call—
the marks across the sand.
Sudden possibilities as the lizard man shudders
on the rock and darts into a canyon
whose name is pronounced Lord.

The Lizard War

He held himself in the light
and told them it was
no longer enough.
The lizards hung by their tails,
changed the air in the room
from green to red to blue.

He punished himself in the night
and taught them to pray
for the dying river, its water
turning gold, slowly disappearing,
its banks hiding the fresh
reptiles that crossed the white
sands in secret.

He waited for himself at dawn,
showed those who were awake
how to pull the tails, twist
the heads off, fry them
without a thought to the poison
that rose in the fire, dotted
the air with the scent of flowers
each of them knew by name.

For the Other World

For those who ran in the streets,
there were no faces to welcome them back.
José escaped and loved the war.

For those who swam with bitterness
of a scorched love,
there was a rusted car to work on.

For those who merely passed
and reclined in prayer,
there were the tower and the cross.

For those who dedicated tongues
to the living and dying,
there were turquiose-painted doorways.

For those who left their children
tied to the water heater,
there were a shout and a name.

For those whose world
was real and beautiful,
there was a cigarette and a saint.

For those who asked José
to stay and feed his children,
there were flowers at their funerals.

For those who carried a shovel
tattooed on their backs,
there were a wet towel and a bottle.

For those who swept the street
of superstition and lie,
there was the turquoise house to come home to.

For those who came home late
and put their swollen feet up,
there were love and the smell of dirty socks.

For those who feared the devil
and spit on his painted arms,
there was a lesson in rosaries.

For those who had to leave
before the sun went down,
there were asphalt and a bus.

For those who stared at wet plaster
and claimed the face of Christ appeared,
there were confinement and stale bread.

For those who talked with each other
and said it was time to go,
there was lead in the paint and on the tongue.

For those who left children behind,
there was a strange world
of sulfur and sparrow nests.

For those who accused their ancestors
of eating salt, there were these hands
tracing what was left after the sweat.

On Guadalupe Street

*in search of the shrine of the Black
Madonna, San Antonio, Texas*

I search for the Black Madonna
hidden on the West Side.
Someone says it is on the East Side.
I don't go there, too late
to see the cistern turn
into a globe of fire.
What remains of the statue
is swallowed by a shaking arm—
the train to the other side of town.

I search for the longhaired, tattooed man
with no shirt, strumming his acoustic guitar,
trying to get out of the way of the needles,
empty beer bottles, homeboys slowly
approaching the sound of his heart.
I look for the Black Madonna and want it
to rise in some dark alley where
pigeon shit and drunkard vomit mark
the way, used condoms contemplating
their colors to match humidity in the air.

I want to see the smooth black marble of the saint,
its stone face frozen in a grip around
my legs that must keep moving,
the cold monument brittle
in the history of vision,
hard in the sweat of mist,
a tale of searching men found
in her folded, draped arms.

*

In the cow pens, there is a frozen heart.
In the music of back rooms, a window.
In the wooden box of the artist,
a mother and father pounding each other,
his bare back glistening with the tattoo
of a blue Virgin, moles and scars vibrating
with the sin of what is holy and indifferent
to the pain of living rooms, the glow
of black-and-white television outlining his love
for naked women, branded bodies, the arms
of his wife lifting to answer him.

In the sweat of her forehead, an image of a thorn,
a time to sing quietly outside the open window.
In the deposited honey behind my ears,
an itch of a small boy not knowing these lovers
came on the torn sofa, came again
and whispered something he didn't understand.

*

I touch rumors of a black breathing,
feel the wires on fences, see empty shrines
in watered gardens, containers of candles
and dried flowers dissolving into
the affliction of angels who disappeared when
this neighborhood was chosen as the site,
the sculptured well where mothers believed
their fasting would end, their suffering
continue, masked men in their beds turning
to love them in silence, love them in shame.

When I approach the hidden well,
graffiti glows on the doors,
pulls doorknobs, and melts glass in my hands.
I find an old car engine humming in the garage,
tire of searching for the altar, and fold
handkerchiefs in that garage all night.
When I want to lay asphalt

on a dirt street to the Madonna,
I run out of black cloth and quietly
leave my country instead.

~~~

José Is Told by La Virgen de Guadalupe He Will Die on a Friday in 110-Degree Heat

He kneels and waits for her to appear.
The empty church punishes him as he prays.
He rises to leave the dark chamber, blown candles
hiding their flames, melting wax frozen in the air.
When José opens the heavy doors to the outside,
it is Friday and the heat has not arrived.
He knows the streets have emptied for him,
cleared the homeboys waiting behind parked cars
to see how José cries in the light of evening.

He stares down at the concrete as he walks,
reminding him of the razor blades
and plastic iguanas hanging by a thread
under his homemade altar—a room to pray
in his sweating mind, a homeless space
following him toward the end of the week
when all men must die.
José pauses before the outdoor shrine—
the smell of roses and gardenias surrounding him
as he kneels and hears La Virgen talk,
her Spanish making him panic,
a sound preceding a blue haze of fire,
the dance his dying mother warned him about.

He kneels in the garden and someone
takes his place on the earth.
The sun grows hotter, streets of El Paso
filling with smoke that escapes through
the green robes of the woman who slips
between stones, takes José toward
a Friday where everyone goes,
all things exploding into rings of flowers,
waves of scorching air welcoming the body song—

the sigh José releases as he falls back
on the wet, cool grass, stares up at
the face of a woman he has loved
greater than his wounded threshold.

I Hear the Bells of the Ice-Cream Vendor
Outside My Door

The sign on his cart says *Pancho's Ice Cream*.
Pifas, my cousin, beats me to the raspa treats,

the ice-cream vendor pushing his cart as I cross the bridge.
The wind knocks me over, lifts me near the cliffs.

A thousand feet below, purple rocks take me
farther away from my early streets.

The sign appears again—Pancho's Ice Cream.
I hear the bells and his cries, *"Paletas! Paletas!"*

The man pushes his cart, leaves me hanging
off the bridge, a tornado striking my mother's house,

ice from snowcones flying across the chasm of fear
as I reach the other side of the bridge.

I wake in the trees of a flavor I never tasted,
my lost cousin dead in Vietnam, bells of the vendor

ringing in my ears as I buy two snowcones—
one for Pifas, one for me, and I eat mine

in darkness as the second drips
strawberry red in my cold hands.

Kiva Floor at Abo

What do I know in my confusion?
How does it shape my legs and arms
as they sink deeper into the earth,
ancient red walls smothering something
I was taught long ago, forgotten words
written in a place I will never look?
If I hear the drum, I am mistaken.
To ask for directions is to pretend
I can identify three or four worlds
where no pumas were trapped
to strengthen this room.

It is the whispering that taught me
how the white dot in the window
is larger than itself—
its dimensions injuring several families
before healing them of ambition.
What if I can't climb out and dirt warnings
explode over my arms?
Skin inside second skin where
the afternoon reveals how far
the wooden ladder goes down.
To descend is to listen.

Climbing back up kills necessity,
shards littering the floor in patterns
I saw when my troubles began.
Though I speak softly, the galaxy
embedded in these old bricks
will not emerge, the search
for the other room a wish
from a god who wants one
full circle of sweating men.

Do I know where to kneel and dig?
Will this desecration last a lifetime,
or will the weight of the blue fly
etched on this stone mean a theft,
a way of bowing down, tasting
the dirt as if water is not water
and greed is fed by shadows moving
to the other side of the eclipse?

⁓

Add Nothing to the Shattered Bird

Add nothing to your hands—close frame
   in possession of beards, arrows,
shields from mistaken souvenirs.

Add opinion to the stem—serious injury
   despite waves of illegals eating breakfast
halfway across the international bridge.

Add eyelashes to the earth's surface—selfish touch
   deciphering which lover left,
which beautiful baptism made her return.

Add sequences to your lips—approved alphabet
   jailing the Spanish tongue to avoid
trapping avocados in future encryptions.

Add meditations itching with rapture—funny horizons
   colored to amuse the calendars left behind
to assure devastation of the barbed wire.

Add train robberies west of downtown—hungry illegals
   stopping the cars and boarding to find
crates and crates of disposable diapers.

Add music to compressed tension—destroyed ribs
   buried by the river to explode when
thousands cross without being turned back.

Add muscular wisdom—faltering ceremonies
   giving birth to computerized babies
already dreaming in English and wanting to go back.

Add scanned knowledge with forgetfulness—cries invented
   to send a message to hovering bandits
spilling out of your headphoned ears.

Add nothing to the shattered bird—lone creature
    that resisted the sun when the sun
was the only desert that burned.

Part Two

Granadilla

Fruit of the passionflower in a secret room.
It has been a long time since a theory of illusion
was accepted by blue herons flying over the city.

Fruit of the exchange sliced into pieces geometrically
entering the body, nourishing the migration of butterflies
to be studied but not tracked down in time.

Fruit of the flower mistaken for angels
and troubled monks who lick their fingers
of the sticky substance, go on with their task

of converting magic into dogma, the juice
of the fruit gathering in clay jars to become
the ballad of the body they were warned about.

Fruit of the harvest given its seed, its esctasy promising
nothing to those desiring more than the pickings from
a trembling branch with its holy hair of the invisible.

Fruit in lavender glass bowls armed with moisture
from the laps of widows, mistaken for the divinity
of prophetic apples, bitten into by ripe ghosts full

of oranges, lemons, and darkening bananas—
yearning passed beyond the evil waters found
in the crushed fruit, the disappointment of finding

the pulp is dangerous overcome by emptying it
into the open mouth, this communion
between the hummingbird and its one prayer.

Field Notes for Diego Rivera

Diego's erased murals reappeared
on the back of a fly in a house in Mexico, 1996.
I swatted it and saw the murals
emblazened on my forehead, the paint
extending down my back, until
I couldn't wash off the weight.

Naked, I stood before the mirror
and learned about Diego's mistakes.
The murals began to sweat as I stared
at the crowds beating on my chest
to have a good look.

I wanted to give the murals back to Diego,
wake him from his nap in the garden.
Frida appeared at my door, her knock
as soft as the heart she held in her hands.
I saw her standing there without opening the door,
knew who she was and did not let her in.

The murals were erased off my body
by the heat of knowing too much.
His great scenes of civilization hated me
and disappeared with Frida, the fly,
the tiny box Diego dedicated before his head
was covered by vines on the porch.

I could breathe again, didn't know what to do
with the paint smeared on my hands.
The murals were erased so Diego could
draw them again in the box he would
leave at the foot of Frida's bed,
as I began to paint the fly glistening
green and blue on the wall.

Commotion

Tiny values cast on the wall.
  Lovers of slim figures caught
in the hum of traffic—imprisoned outline
  of an old farmhouse
in the microscopic painting—
  even fingernails hold more galleries
than what is here.

The crowd breaks windows and enters,
  cigarette lighters in their eyes,
small flames already
  searching for conquest.
When the swans stay perfectly
  still in the water, an architecture
is found on the walls of the mansion.

Normal beliefs have value.
  Seventeen forefingers tracing cilantro
are not enough to believe
  there is a strong scent
coming from a place of danger.
  A nodding trumpet player
clicking his fingers to the beat.

Great philosophies taking the wheel.
  In front of news cameras,
two conditions being set forth—
  one for the edge of town,
the second for commissioned laughter
  escaping the eye of the lens.

Massive thinking weaving through
  ambassadors sampling fine cigars
in dark smoke shops as their mistresses
  mount other men in hotels.

When the dust of snow says it is noon,
    commotion is rapidly disappearing
around the corner of a wooden box
    where antique cuff links are kept,
the price of their keeping
    allowing the owner to wager
against those who would take
    the shiniest ones and sell them
to finance trouble on the streets.

Federico García Lorca's Desk

It was tied with guitar strings
into a sack that held pigeon feathers,
the hair of lost dogs—cardboard
from a box of trinkets
he received from North Africa.
García Lorca's desk was a bundle
of things bearing down like an easy shot,
words recalled when discontent
was a shade of black,
coffee beans stolen in silence—
a clock over the hills waiting
for the next moon.

García Lorca's desk was a head
of lettuce, a bowl of goat soup,
the place where tiny hands
were named for their fingers,
ink spotting the pages to buy time
before three doors were slammed.
García Lorca's desk was his vow
to stir the rain with rootless awe,
then hide for years, come out
singing, reciting poems
from the warmth of laps,
paper flattened on the desk
so the sun could read.

García Lorca's desk was found
decaying in an empty field
where they lined him up,
the feathers falling out,
guitar strings rounding the sky
with wired light that sank

into the soft paper he used
to wipe his hands
before he was shot.

~~~

Black Flowers

They paste black flowers on the wall,
turn oblivion into a stream from my hands
that no longer hold a seductive god
who mimics me before I think of him again.

Someday the arch of stones will be torn down
to reveal the skeleton of my grandfather,
his white hands holding a stubborn root
lining his grave to the cottonwood.

This lone thought drips water
in the acequia at San Elizario,
the irrigation canal carrying liquid
to the burning houses, hundreds

of Tewa Indians dying at the church door,
my Spanish priest watching people fall
as he listens—black flowers etched
into the sanctuary wall.

Someday they will call me, diabolic antlers
erased from the unfinished drawing,
my fingers tracing them with charcoal,
the artist standing behind me,

knife at my back as he guides my hands over
the old map, and I wonder if my throat
will burst before I trace the black petal
that always sends him away.

Robert Desnos in My Mother's Garden

for George Kalamaras

He comes out of his trance
and knows where he is,
finds me standing there
and nods his head—azalea look,
rose posture, magnolia shape
crusting over blackberry brows,
Desnos growing in my mother's garden,
planted there by the wish I had
when the future was a room of leaves,
years I had no soul forgiven by
the yellow grass, installed there
by Desnos's sleeping sweat,
murmurs in gardens of the past
drying up with him.

He waters my mother's violets,
the stream trickling out of
his body, draining him with
magical repose, fertilizing families
with silent lips he moves but
I can't hear, the hanging willow
turning orange as Desnos floats
across the brick path, settles
into the blackberries again
like a difficult translation I can
hardly read, his closed eyes hidden
in the thorns, juice from broken berries
staining his mind, reducing him
to the closed eyes of what drips
down his chin when I wake up
in the empty kitchen.

See This

I opened my hand and the spider
was there, throbbing in the light
as if I were the last son crying
over things I had recalled.
The spider disappeared as I turned,
curtains falling across my back
when I moved the window and it rained.
I shook my arm and the spider flew,
wet air thriving in my eyes—
slow motion of anger filling me with
the day when I could please the sun,
bury clouds across the sky as if meaning
were here and I could tattoo blue lines
across my face. The mask pulled me
toward Carlos Manzano's *Child
With Hidden Arms*, the painting
where the boy carries a secret in his heart,
arms hidden behind the candle flames,
a voice and future standing behind him
to make sure his arms never touch another,
only grow muscles within the family
of spiders who pray to walls,
webs of love and hair dotting the windows
to keep the boy from escaping to the road.
I stared, shook my arms so the alphabet
of spiders appeared on my wrists,
their love for me keeping me from
the light in the painting, whispers
behind calling me to stop thinking
about the boy with no arms, his need
to wave them, dance the fire we swallow
when those who keep us from shining
sketch their charcoal across our garden
of plants where baby spiders are hatching
and already flexing their legs.

The Standing Fossil at Yuccati

Say it is there, changing over time
to become your rhythm,
arms and body of rock fierce against
the tracings of the eye, time pulling
it out of the ground to survive.
Say it is bound toward the horizon,
visitors gazing at their own preservation,
trying to understand why the sun skipped a day
to release a pattern—the perfect way
to step into the world.

*

Every few minutes, I breathe
like a man drinking tea.
Each moment encircles water to form drops
anchored against the skin—a brown hue
of sweat and soreness found
in the history of escape.
When I ran, I came here.
When I saw what wanted to come out
of the ground, it was raining.
One body told me I had to see.

*

Say it is the morning of exploration,
the day of stone linguistics,
knotted fire of what does not speak.
When you study it,
you stand in the right moment,
sand overcoming your shoes,
a sudden haze of black wasps moving
you closer to the slab fighting
to right itself against what you know.

*

No one talks to me.
The shape of talk would kill these walls.
No one wants to see.
When I was born, this road did not exist.
When I was a child wanting to find
what fell in the arroyo,
these hands had been digging
for five hundred years.

No one talks to me.
There is writing on the far wall.
It must be held that I never understood.
I must say each word quietly,
practice the sound of sand.

*

Say it is the day of the dawning figure.
Find its form and say a wish.
Take the ton of rock with you
as if you could move the earth.
It is the last chance to trace the story
before the lines and circles become
one direction you have never been.
When you shape the handle
of the next thing you build,
call it this.
Say it several times and never dig.
When they finally let this thing stand up,
it will be easy to make a wish.

Facing the Reef, Guadalupe Mountains

Fissure rising thousands of feet,
old sea taking its time lighting fires.
When they inserted radio transmitters
into twenty mountain lions,
these canyons ended their silence.
When they released them, I came back,
saw the massive cut in the wall
before it came down.

Why the face would rather be the river
changing wilderness into maps of escape.
Inside the mountain reef, a dance of shells.
Outside their chambers, miles
of unknown forest spreading
toward its underground heart.

In this cottonwood break, a broken claw.
Above the towering red cliffs,
the place where things erupt,
taking the horizon to its source—
the spot where I stand to leave.

What it took to open my eyes
above the breathing fossils.
The chance to turn the transmitter on.
No one to listen to the beeping stream
flow to the other side of leaving.
Sandstone petrifying the red scratch
between one word and the one lion.

Cave Swallows, Carlsbad Caverns

It is raining birds as we descend,
the black entrance spreading wings.
Swallows bend and hide in the walls,
leap into the air to ribbon the light
with streaks and shadows, the moment
vanishing in the sudden cave.

Birds of silence and superstition.
Not a sound is heard as we stop
and look up, the tunnel pulling
our legs, reminding me it is said
if you pause before a cave,
you know what came before you—
how the earth opened in search
of itself, a flock of swallows hurtling
into the sky before the first person
ever found this hole.

Birds of rock and the covered mound.
Sandstone walls pockmarked with nests.
Same birds that left my hands
the last time I came here.
They are gone and return,
the trail leading into a tunnel where
no swallow follows without becoming
lost again—the dream where
we are never found three miles
below the earth, flying blind
to the bottomless pit where
a blue light is the only pure
nest of our habitation.

~

The Hawk Temple at Tierra Grande

I climbed the rocky slope and saw it—
the hawk temple in the trees,
feathers hanging on arrows
someone fired into the bark.

I came closer and found the hawk
perched there, waiting,
its black head the eye of the messenger,
its wings the color of my skin.

I stood under the tied trees,
wondered who did this—
why they lashed the mighty pines
together with rope,

binding the hawk to its perch,
leaving it there to blink
and stare at me as if
I was going to climb the tree.

I got too close and it tried
to fly, its talons cutting
into the branch, unable
to free itself from the rope.

I turned to run when I heard
a sound—a cry I hear to this day,
a motion of air to keep me
from saying what I do not say,

the sight of the hawk temple
not telling me if I will find
what I am looking for,
its screech not sounding
as though it will be freed.

Pink Railroad Cars at Los Mochis

Who painted them completely pink?
Who left three boxcars on tracks
through the cottonfields of mist?
Bright pink railroad cars rusting in the valley
of bent backs, fleeing men, broken journeys
ending in a battle over salt, an encounter
over the flooded canals that watered these crops
before the pink railroad cars stopped at the gates.
When you pause to look at their long pink sides,
there is no sunrise without danger,
no stone in a pasture full of wooden ties
piled to keep the river away.
Pink railroad cars without sound or hitch,
their paint looking fresh and luminous
against cottonwoods that listen for smoke,
turn green with lettuce and the fault
of an invisible martyr dropping boxcars
like crushed bone against smooth flesh.
Who took the time to make them pink?
Who chose the color and laughed at this?
In Los Mochis, territory is marked in blood
and given a chance to harvest the fields.
In town, the train no longer stops
to pick up the prisoners or deliver the goats.
The last time the locomotive arrived,
a fire had destroyed the station and pecan groves
grew out of the ashes.

*

Pink railroad cars fall into the river.
Too many people have come to take a look,
the pink light of amazement locked
in cold, deep chambers under the fields.
Remember the pink boxcars at Los Mochis?

Climb out of the cotton and lettuce and take a look.
There is a pink iron bridge spanning the border,
its color taking the men away, its twisted wheels
rusting in the air above the angry river.

~

Cristo Viene Pronto

Cristo Viene Pronto ("Christ Comes
Soon"): *graffiti on a portable-toilet door,*
downtown El Paso.

He comes only once, dying pigeons
in San Jacinto Plaza getting out of his way.

The doors of every toilet stall fly open
as construction stops downtown.

Cristo tears the streets apart, looks for the drunks
he saved one hundred years ago,

shaves the head of every homeless man in sight,
taking them into the alley one by one, the songs

they learn from him the oaths recited
by Tewa Indians hanged in the plaza long ago.

Cristo viene pronto and no one knows
how to eat their menudo of miracles,

red chili that makes you sit in the stall.
When he arrives, the rainstorm washes city streets

where the Tewa woman with no legs
pushes herself on wheels against the red light.

Cristo wakes and it doesn't rain;
the *mejicano* who sees him is the first

to make the sign of the cross when the city
locks the toilets, the believer pulling

his zipper down in the alley as he pisses
and prays for another open door.

~~~

Hermitage

One flew and the other vanished
into the books, the great amplifier
of hope needing something to hold
on to—a fish, some potato chips,
the frozen spider on their most
cherished piece of wood—
broken passion in the yucca plant
making room for the explosion
of the barrel cactus.

One sat down and waited for
the pieces to fly into his brain,
reincarnate him as the city in
the tumbleweed that rolls away.
The other came home a forgotten
hero, his tattoos vanishing the instant
he walked into the house,
his brother looking up and
mistaking him for a prowler,
telling him to see how it feels
to be lifted into heaven.

One suffered, the other disappeared
into the manuscript in the cottonwood,
their names borrowed for
street signs, happy festivals, boarded-
up buildings where homeless men
stuttered and wondered why
the shelter gave them T-shirts
with bullet holes in them,
this story extracted from the books
found under the tree after
it was cut down by two boys
in search of fresh fruit.

Rumors

Rumors visited and rumors left alone
to suspend imagination as a savage foot
stuck between rails in abandoned train yards,
no engine charging, no train going back,
the man of insistence watching dead whales
accepted into the wreckage where
he used to be a short-order cook.
He knows the human head, frees himself
from the yard, runs toward the snowflakes
filling his rented room with possessions
he thought he threw away—
a broken comb, the key to a hotel,
an old baseball he gripped each time
he opened the door and left.
Rumors of explosive cells heaving
through the wet chest of a man in
a dripping shower where other naked
men watch him wake up, hand him
a bar of soap, leave him to dry himself
in a prison chamber one thousand miles
from the nearest road.

Rumors beyond the evening breast as
he gathers the taste of sulfur in his mouth,
arrives in the valley of danger where
surviving mules ride out of the slaughter
to rip Picasso's *Guernica* off the walls.
From where he stands, it is a battle,
a dance, the mathematics of spit spraying
the North Star with forgiveness.
Rumors despite the keeper of his name,
coming home to find his wife consuming
another man, their twisting bodies reaming
the room with the betrayed man's last attempt
to say it isn't so as his potion flower

diminishes into hawk claws, feeds
livers of moss to his eleven children
before their mother gives birth again,
vines in the teeth of their scarecrow
whispering beyond the lanterns of a fool.

Calle de Colon, Mesilla

Nothing about walking,
dirt street introduced by itself,
swollen worms falling out of the trees,
wriggling on the sidewalk like ribbons
for the night when my shadow enters
the hacienda as though I lived there.
Everything against crossing the street
where men with drawn swords
appear in the cottonwoods,
the blood of their wisdom ringing
in the acequia, water from here and there,
irrigation for the homeless and the rich
hiding in renovated, haunted houses.

Corners of wrong things and finely kept stone.
Flowers and shrines where nothing is new,
the scent of a clean road pleasing the owner
who comes out of his house,
stares at me as I go by, goes inside
when I turn to him and nod,
crossed antlers of an elk swinging
quietly from his barest tree.

Nothing about knowing this place
like a dream that never was, those
rock fences and prickly pear gardens
blinding me in the early evening,
gravel in the dirt street spread evenly
like the horizon where something happened—
someone made a choice and houses vanished—
empty lots protecting their flat light,
covering a site where something burned,
someone cried, "Go away. Come back.
Don't return. This is where we live."

Nothing about moving farther from
the wish to touch a house where
someone opens the door, shows me
the dust where I was born, confusion
in the grass nothing but a bench to sit on,
the closest yellowjacket hovering
too far for me to wave it away,
one second under this willow
one dream without the heat.
Nothing about memory, the rain
in the mudrooms removing my clothes,
setting me in the stone tub
where I stayed for years, this empty lane
the long arm of the one who pulled
me out, dried my back, whispered,
"These are the houses with the lighted windows
you have been looking for,"
a glow where someone waits,
where backyards loom with a way to flee,
to come back here after that escape,
sit upon the closing stone as I choose
one house, one door that opens to let me in.

What You Will Remember

The blue stone in the palm of the hand.
The orange held between the breasts.
A hawk dead in the middle of the road.
The dry tree bursting through the adobe.

The half-burned church in Chamberino
blackened and open to the sky.
A field of cotton with two men running across.
The saint in the window.

The road to Cochiti and the pass
to the last desert town.
The red stone from the agate beach,
hundreds of seabirds disappearing
beyond the island of fog.

No one in the window.
The smell of chorizo frying in the air,
sound of a lone gunshot across the night.
The dog dead in the middle of the road.

The eagle flying above the car
outside the ruins at Abo.
A green stone worn around the neck
as the mango is sliced to be eaten.

The river drying, reappearing within hours.
An old woman carrying a broken wooden chair,
a hedge of enormous cactus blocking her house,
green and white streamers blowing on telephone poles.

The barbed wire surrounding the church.
A huge lizard on the fence at the rest stop.
The closed eyes of La Virgin.
A man mistaken for a ghost crossing the road.

The headlights of a distant tractor.
Hands rubbing a headstone again and again.
The lacquered shoes on the bookshelf from
a tiny baby who never made it.

Part Three

I Am Afraid of the Moon

I am afraid of the moon when it comes down
to touch my throat, its light weaving
the white vein into my heart,
its brief cycle shimmering with evidence
that I have been wrong.

I am afraid of the moon when the toads
have become extinct, their legs deformed
into red spiders that drown their voices,
moonlight exploding in the water
to warn me I am still wrong.

I fear the full moon above the mountains,
its yellow wash the gold left behind by
men who loved night skies with stars,
their ancestors mistaken when they believed
there was no earth to flee to without
the light of their shadows falling into
their tombs to wash their toes.
That time the moon was wrong.

I do not trust the moon when
everything is gone, my companions from
the translucent land fleeing the cycles
of madness long ago, their terrible cries
beyond the seasons bringing them back
by the quarter-moon where they try
to catch one dimension, but can't
separate it from the bloodless sky.

I am afraid of the moon because
it changes my home each time it arrives,
its dangling power ignored for a few nights

before the desert floor becomes a storm where
those of us blinded at birth by moonlight
don't know what it is like to be wrong.

Round

Forgive me for the collection of marbles in my pocket.
They were gathered for years, some falling out
of my elbows when my body was wearing down.
I tried to smell truthful, but all I had was greed.
Even without my blessing of mint, I was happy
with my way of talking to the shadows.

When I stopped my car at the busy intersection,
the woman in the car next to me was saying a rosary,
holding the beads in one hand, her eyes
on the traffic light, lips trembling.
I thought of the marbles, how I had not rubbed them
in prayer because prayer was inside me.

You who will not believe me,
it was only a woman in a car saying a rosary.
I swear I saw it and it frightened me.
When I quit believing, I saw the fields move
and thought it was the day I waited for.
You who will insist on shaking your head,
let me tell you about the tall grass flattened
by the wind like in a movie, a bad novel,
the hill where a chopped onion rolled past my feet.

Only Once

When I returned from the myth of my mother's hair,
I saw a brilliant needle of light land on her shoulders.

I turned away as her son, but she motioned me into her garden
and pointed to her willow tree.

When I looked at the cascading branches, the light in her body vanished.
When I shook my head, she was gone.

All I had was a pile of pages and a name for a new god,
an asking and a gift where no one gets hurt, no one composes

with a twisted leg, for a willow that grows its own history
without spreading across the tired world.

I saw an old woman once and she did not ask anything of me,
an old woman who came back as the brown skin on my shoulder.

It was too early for me to know what the dripping magnolia means—
a wish to love the blackberry bush as I cut my fingers on its sticky fruit,

standing there years after the willow
and my mother disappeared.

I gathered the rain, drop by drop, formed a sign with my hands
and let it fall, waited for the moon to turn into a leaf.

I no longer asked for a dust storm, counted wasp nests above the porch
        door,
ignored the sound of dying in a house being cleaned of ghosts.

I left too late to see that my secret tree was the mountain's skull,
moved too late to find how far this meaning flares a candle,

calls the flame by its names—illusion, fire, yellow eye of confession,
and faith with its limitations.

This is how a new willow was replanted, imagination asking
for a brown breast to take my language,

forgive the shattered glass of autumn
as the last time I made it across the water.

~~~

You Are

You are the goat in the road, the string of blood
hiding inside the basket of the wrong woman.
You are the sandstorm, its embrace
of dust spilling the past over torn roads.
You are the face in the tumbleweed,
the mustard dropped in the sandwich—
far cry from the sign on the building
announcing no one is there.

You are the hand of the drummer tapping
on the back of a misused car lot,
the lot boy washing vehicles
in one-hundred-and-ten-degree heat.
You are his sweat, his smell chasing
summer flies away from windshields
reflecting faces of sorry salesmen
cashing in on the poverty of their lives.

You are the crowd on the street corner
where the young boy saw his dead mother
standing three days after she died,
the body buried in the desert so no one
could find the boundary between
the dry stalk of an old sunflower
and a new weed left unnamed.

~~~

Rutaya

Rutaya: the legend of the power of the first woman any man falls in love with.

Night and you can hear music.
Small victories occur.
It is what the horizon brings.
Small hunger, smaller embraces,
the decision to keep the boys
from going into the volcano.
Here are the secret passengers.
Let them wake before they laugh.
Tell them, "Listen to your blood and Rutaya arrives."

Rutaya of the open book.
Rutaya who could have seen the stars, but didn't.
She holds the river, but the boys have to be
loyal to her screams, her body,
her hair of a thousand miles and one rope of trust.
She pulls the mouse out of one boy's ear
and shows him it is the dove of his dreams.
Rutaya washes her hands of their fathers' voices,
vanishes as they turn from men into trees.

Nothing is pungent and lost.
Nothing loves the smile of Rutaya as her bald slave.
He waits for her to fire his misfortune with a song,
a dish of cow tongue, the last pear from the bowl
she broke when she returned.
No one dreams of a scaled fish.
Few men know how to hook that streak
and admit their daughters are beautiful.

Rutaya as the unclaimed daughter of such lies.
Rutaya resurrected as anything a man can say.
When she was announced, no shadow played,

no men died, not a single tale of granite was believed.
When the other women emerged into the streets,
the town changed its name and I was born.

Falling into a Face

It would be strange to fall into a face and never return.
That lone hawk chasing my car along
the mountain road would disappear.

How magnificent it would be
to fall into a face and be loved.
I could kiss the nipples of a startled girl

and know she would eventually love me.
I would be the first boy discovering the face
inside the face that prowls between

the joined bodies of two young lovers.
It would be here for me to fall
into a face and gain.

I would see how the world
is eaten by the rains that fall out
of the face that holds my face

in its hands, its cold fingers brushing
the water from my eyelids,
taking me deeper into the musk

I don't know—startled scent
of a face announcing the face
at the window is the same profile

that turns gently within the body,
moving out of the heart
as I fall into a face and see.

Savior

I look into the eyes of loved women.
I kneel and pray each week.
The difficult bird flutters out of my navel.

I'm going somewhere else.
I'm going somewhere drumming.
I don't know if it is spoken about—

When the bird leaves, I have two legs.
When I turn, I am loved.
When I stop, I'm going somewhere to be handled

by icy trees, streets that cry,
and nights that come to me
in three languages.

Kick the Heart

Kick the heart.
Kick the starting lance.
Throw the ground a word and stand back.
The color of terror is the envy
on body rags, the dragonfly war
scraped off a painting inside the door.

Kick the shame.
Kick the falling dawn as fortunate.
Throw the corrupted guest out the door.
A sequence of rhythms bounds for
the light on your bed.
On the eggplant cooked for the husband
working late: an ant, a hair—
the only thing said to race the mind.
Take someone else's voice and touch their ears.
Make sure they hear you cry
in their own whispers, their harangue.

Kick the soil.
Kick the sweet drowning as if you know
the round jubilance of pear is afraid
of a darkening spoon, a honey of flavor,
the tender one who never touches your plate.
Kick the tired one who rations food
to thank God eternity is here and there.

Slip the eye of the blue-black stranger,
his instrument of scars and neglect,
its tune of every wish beside
the grave of a careless, quiet man.
Shape his sound into the thumb asking
for a ride in the years of not going anywhere.

Kick the alphabet.
Kick the hungry thigh and try again.
Reduce yourself to a moving mouth, a solemn happiness
that smells of the past, takes hold of the throat,
and teaches you to despise omens—
ignore Apache mirrors on rock arches
as if you knew what their scratchings meant.

Kick the heart.
Kick the starting lance.
It moves deeper into the mouth of blinking neon
where vertigo is perfume, desire foaming
on your bare feet killed by frost,
taken by the animal waking inside your holy cross—
a figure of green gowns and things
that follow you until you dance.

Kick the truth.
Kick the belly until it confesses.
Admit you were fed by a woman
flapping in the wind, told to sit there by a father
who made her give birth to a shimmering head,
your brain of flowers blossoming upon
the body always first to confess.

What snow is left is tired water unmoved by your
seasonal words, your circle healing by slowing down,
swelling to the size of God,
yellow leaves in the blood nothing dangerous—
this impulse, this kick to the brittle lake
where the snow goes away.

One World

Think of the green stem as a necklace—
   the light that kills desire does not belong.
A black cricket in the mouth of the cat,
   the blind boy defeating the neighborhood.
Think of a solution that suffers ten billion cells,
   the doves that move on the fence.
Ask the old couple walking by.

The way they worship the light,
   a manner in which they improvise.
The way they thank the world
   for the lines on their hands,
roads, and mouths for what doesn't arrive.
   The skill of walking by the doves
without startling them into flight.

Think of love as lyric practice—
   a sense of absent time does not heal.
Needles in the red tree equal darkness as
   a man is finally able to talk to his father.
Faith as distance between whispers and stones.
   Take a kiss on the cheek and say "Amen."
Weep lust into folded hands without lifting your eyes.

The way you spin crushed herbs in the air,
   how it creates an aroma.
Look at yourself each day,
   sleep and her name singing
for what has never left you.
   The way of standing by the water
without searching for rescue or myth.

The Hand

The hand takes the time to warm the beetle
inside the carved wood.
There is no going back when
the candles are blown out.

When you read about the pollen of winter,
your tears are clowns.
There is barbed wire flying
across the fruit of laughter.

The hand becomes the time the beetle
consumes inside the carved wood.
There is a talent screaming inside
the layers of a borrowed onion.

No one cares about this
or will denounce what is being said.
There are times when a door made of lilies
bleeds a thousand miles from home.

The hand trembles the time it takes
to warm the moving beetle.
There is a blind apricot chasing
the diameter of a careful fingerprint.

The hand digs out the beetle
from the wood.
There is an identical image
answering for the second time.

When you strike the vowel
and travel beyond a mongrel dog's ear,
there is a tiny chalice of blood
blessing you with a borrowed kiss.

The hand is the warm beetle
rising out of the carved wood.
There are a few seconds
when the beetle tastes good.

~

Posing in the Light on Kenneth Rexroth's Birthday, December 22

I pose in the light and laugh.
I have loved many things for too long,
plotted escape past the hands of a music
without thought, without knowing
the century will never end.

I pose in a light not fed by stars,
not seen by most, bought and given back
upon opening the sky and cold.
Light not torn by secrets, unblinking
in the blinding note, tossed into
the wings of sparrows, mistaken
for the flight of doves.

I stand in the glare and see,
shudder at the size of the mirror
engaged in power, in giving me
a way to take the blaze, send it
past the gift of knowing
this is the profile and those
the hands refocusing without
asking for a smile.

Light not fed by stars,
unnamed and forgiven, taken
and insured against wrong roads.
Light not asked to be light,
left here for me to pose and think
that this is the first day beyond that light.

The Horse's Eye

after a photograph by Susan Unterberg

Magnified and shut, the horse's eye resembles
a parchment from my father's lies

told to us when he was done
with the woman on the street,

microscopic sadness in the photo building
out of the crushed horse's face,

its surface so close to the lens,
there is no way out of the ride.

Turning the blowup the other way,
a female moth rises out of the skin,

wrinkled like the moment my father aged,
his face buried between the hooker's thighs.

The horse's eye is so invasive,
its vision is passed from captor to captor,

as in the days when people could
alight inside each other's mind,

their perch dissolving into quarrels
and sacrifices to the Palino god—

the power with six eyes on his head,
dozens of tiny men and women

pouring out of his mouth
to find their way over the earth.

The lone horse's eye in the photo is
the halo we were granted when we were born,

the ring of love our mothers threw up
when they could no longer bleed.

Opening my eyes to look again: sunlight
and the hoof pressing down her spine.

~

The Alley

Even as I looked up,
there was a miracle in the alley.
When I moved from there,
the asphalt softened.
Angry boys walked through at night,
letting the sleeping neighborhood know
the color in their eyes had nothing to do
with comfortable dreams.

If I were someone from far away,
I would stare at this city for too long.
I was not from here and wanted to know
how these streets became paths to the other side.

Waking next to the last leaf in the alley,
I was afraid of a delicate turnover—
a quiet style of moving.
Something made me stop to listen
and take myself back.
It was quiet beyond the border.
When I stepped there,
the mountains were beautiful
and my father was draped in robes.

Back

Explain the truth: these stones are not ornaments.
Explain the truth: my brother comes home with a twisted leg.

He is a twisted leg,
truthful and solid with pain.

Tell the truth: say stupid things to rhyme with scorn.
There will be stupid things to eat and kiss for the brain.

The day grins on the road misused.
The power to shake castanets and look like a fool.

Say the truth: the spine on the naked back of the woman.
There will be ways to slow down.

She is the love of the shape,
the one with the hands that teach.

No one wants to say the words "Go on."
No one believes there is a raised glass.

Again, the truth: basic situation with borrowed clouds.
When the man hammers the wood, the house is done.

To each pair of hands, a gift.
To the one who wants a different tree, a leaf.

To mistake the last spider for an easy thought.
To have thought it through and received a bright-colored bead.

The delicate and twisted leg of my brother.
The way family owns memory.

Explain the truth: white walls, white floors.
Brown foot shredding the sand with prayers.

No one inhales when my brother comes near.
No one moves or says a word.

There is a chance to explain why everyone left.
There is junction, turn, commission, and greed.

To have seen the willow in the yard.
To have known the broken fence.

To have mistaken my brother for a lone survivor.
To have been slow and quiet.

Tell the truth: backyards and the spinning dusk of the river.
Backyards and the last place where we told the truth.

My Earliest Memory

I am flying through the air,
held up as a one-year-old
in my grandmother's right hand,
her arm straight up
as she lies in her bed,
trying to make me quit crying.

She made me fly every night,
my eyes staring at the votive candles
flickering on the nightstand
as if I knew something about the flames,
this joyful play at night
meaning I would see things
from above before I would
set my tiny feet on the ground
for the first time.

Giggling and flying;
my grandmother holding me up
by one strong hand,
telling me the boy who flies
will sleep better once
he leaves the earth.

What the Cottonwood Said

after James Wright

Don't witness the river changing course.
It is not good to stand here,

your mind crying: *This birth of mine*
never came from the darkness.

Don't measure the height of the clouds
with a dream. No one else

will cross the water without you.
Be there when my leaves dry up,

when the burlap sack full of shoes
drops under the shade of my trunk,

your missing pair floating down the current
to reach your resting place before you do.

*

Cottonwood shadows turning on me,
a sign was carved on your trunk.
When I carried you with me,
everything changed.

The freedom of the sparrows
and your huge, broken limbs.
If I stepped beyond your height,
there would be water—a way to explain.

My blessing is not a wish,
but the spice being tasted—

your leaves, their odor of silence.
I will not speak when I sample
the branch that falls at my feet.

Cottonwood closing the eyes of rivers,
there is a word or two about rain.
When I get wet, scars on your bark
are the clean breaks of a happy man.
How I wish it would rain.

This way of gaining two feet—
a steady hand on your lowest limb
as I listen to the swaying wind.
When I quit talking,
there will be your great height
and my childhood, again.

*

When the lights in the neighborhood go out,
the tree smiles and I wait for the cool air

of early September to turn against me,
chill the hour beyond tomorrow

so I can watch the tree burn with age.
When the first orange leaves touch my face,

I wake and tell the truth:
The debut of shadows will pass beyond me.

One kind of cruelty enlarges the eyes.
There is this tree for order,

a beautiful thumb pressing
against the bark.

When the tree stops smiling,
the greater singing will have begun.

〜

Acknowledgments

The author thanks the following publications in which these poems appeared:

Alaska Quarterly Review: "My Earliest Memory";

Bellview Literary Review: "Rutaya";

The Best American Poetry 2000, edited by Rita Dove (Scribner): "For the Other World";

The Bitter Oleander: "Field Notes for Diego Rivera," "Only Once," "Posing in the Light on Kenneth Rexroth's Birthday, December 22," "See This," "The Alley," "The Lizard War," "There Will Be Centuries," "You Are," "I Am Afraid of the Moon," and "Kiva Floor at Abo";

Black Moon: "Round";

The Café Review: "Tiny Clay Doll with No Arms" and "I Hear the Bells of the Ice-Cream Vendor Outside My Door";

Colorado Review: "The Hawk Temple at Tierra Grande";

Conduit: "Commotion," "The Hand," and "The Scorpions of Coronado";

Crab Orchard Review: "For the Other World";

Denver Quarterly: "On Guadalupe Street";

Electronic Poetry Review: "Add Nothing to the Shattered Bird";

Flyway: "Abo National Monument, New Mexico";

Guild Complex 25th Anniversary Anthology (Tia Chucha Press): "It Was a Turtle";

Homestead Review: "Hermitage" and "Time Capsule";

Kestrel: "The Standing Fossil at Yuccati";

Luna: "Birthday" and "Erosion";

New Orleans Review: "What You Will Remember"

North Stone Review: "Facing the Reef, Guadalupe Mountains" and "The Wide-Open Eyes of the Cathedrals";

Red Rock Review: "Rumors";

Seneca Review: "Federico García Lorca's Desk";

6,500 Magazine: "Onmo";

Snowapple: "Time Capsule";

Sun Dog: "Pink Railroad Cars at Los Mochis," "Lizard Man," "Fray Marcos de Niza Erects a Cross at Hawikah (Zuñi Pueblo), 1539," "José Is Told by La Virgen de Guadalupe He Will Die on a Friday in 110-Degree Heat," and "Falling into a Face";

Terra Nova: "Back";

Touching the Fire: Fifteen Poets of Today's Latino Renaissance (Anchor/Doubleday): "Savior";

The U.S. Latino Review: "Black Flowers" and *"Cristo Viene Pronto"*;

Verse: "What You Will Remember."

I would like to thank The Pike's Peak Writer's Retreat, The Loft Studio Program, and The Corporation of Yaddo for time and space to write. Acknowledgment goes to The University of Minnesota, Twin Cities, for a McKnight Land-Grant Professor fellowship and a President's Research Grant, which gave me valuable support for travel in the desert Southwest.

About the Author

Ray Gonzalez is a poet, essayist, and editor born in El Paso, Texas. He is the author of seven books of poetry, including *The Heat of Arrivals* (BOA, 1996), which won the Josephine Miles Book Award for Excellence in Literature, and *Cabato Sentora* (BOA, 1999). Gonzalez received a 2001 Minnesota Book Award for *Turtle Pictures* (University of Arizona Press), and he has published his first book of fiction, *The Ghost of John Wayne and Other Stories* (University of Arizona Press). He is the editor of twelve anthologies, and he is poetry editor of *The Bloomsbury Review* and editor of *LUNA*, a journal of poetry and translations. Among his awards are a 2001 Loft Literary Center Career Initiative Fellowship, a 1998 Fellowship in Poetry from the Illinois Arts Council, a 1993 Before Columbus American Book Award for Excellence in Editing, and a 1998 Colorado Governor's Award for Excellence in the Arts. Mr. Gonzalez lives in Minneapolis, Minnesota.

BOA EDITIONS, LTD.

AMERICAN POETS CONTINUUM SERIES

No. 1   *The Fuhrer Bunker: A Cycle of Poems in Progress*
        W. D. Snodgrass

No. 2   *She*
        M. L. Rosenthal

No. 3   *Living With Distance*
        Ralph J. Mills, Jr.

No. 4   *Not Just Any Death*
        Michael Waters

No. 5   *That Was Then: New and Selected Poems*
        Isabella Gardner

No. 6   *Things That Happen Where There Aren't Any People*
        William Stafford

No. 7   *The Bridge of Change: Poems 1974–1980*
        John Logan

No. 8   *Signatures*
        Joseph Stroud

No. 9   *People Live Here: Selected Poems 1949–1983*
        Louis Simpson

No. 10 *Yin*
        Carolyn Kizer

No. 11 *Duhamel: Ideas of Order in Little Canada*
        Bill Tremblay

No. 12 *Seeing It Was So*
        Anthony Piccione

No. 13 *Hyam Plutzik: The Collected Poems*

No. 14 *Good Woman: Poems and a Memoir 1969–1980*
        Lucille Clifton

No. 15 *Next: New Poems*
        Lucille Clifton

No. 16 *Roxa: Voices of the Culver Family*
        William B. Patrick

No. 17 *John Logan: The Collected Poems*

No. 18 *Isabella Gardner: The Collected Poems*

No. 19 *The Sunken Lightship*
        Peter Makuck

No. 20 *The City in Which I Love You*
        Li-Young Lee

No. 21 *Quilting: Poems 1987–1990*
        Lucille Clifton

No. 22 *John Logan: The Collected Fiction*

No. 23 *Shenandoah and Other Verse Plays*
        Delmore Schwartz

No. 24 *Nobody Lives on Arthur Godfrey Boulevard*
        Gerald Costanzo

No. 25 *The Book of Names: New and Selected Poems*
        Barton Sutter

No. 26 *Each in His Season*
        W. D. Snodgrass

No. 27 *Wordworks: Poems Selected and New*
        Richard Kostelanetz

No. 28 *What We Carry*
        Dorianne Laux

No. 29 *Red Suitcase*
        Naomi Shihab Nye

No. 30 *Song*
        Brigit Pegeen Kelly

No. 31 *The Fuehrer Bunker: The Complete Cycle*
        W. D. Snodgrass

No. 32 *For the Kingdom*
        Anthony Piccione

No. 33 *The Quicken Tree*
        Bill Knott

No. 34 *These Upraised Hands*
        William B. Patrick

No. 35 *Crazy Horse in Stillness*
        William Heyen

No. 36 *Quick, Now, Always*
        Mark Irwin

Colophon

The publication of *The Hawk Temple at Tierra Grande*, by Ray Gonzalez,
was made possible by the special support
of the following individuals:

Laure-Anne Bosselaar & Kurt Brown
Dr. Henry & Beverly French
Kip & Deb Hale
Robert & Willy Hursh
Dorothy & Henry Hwang
Boo Poulin
Deborah Ronnen
Annette & Aaron Satloff
Jane Schuster
Pat & Michael Wilder

This book was typeset by Richard Foerster, York Beach, Maine,
using Monotype Dante fonts with Arabesque Ornaments.
The cover design is by Lisa Mauro / Mauro Design.
The cover art, "Luz Misteriosa," is by Fernando Mercado,
courtesy of the artist. The author photo is by Lida Steven.
Manufacturing was by McNaughton & Gunn, Saline, Michigan.